POEMS OF PRAISE

by
Carolyn M. G. Fletcher

AuthorHouse™
1663 Liberty Drive
Bloomington, IN 47403
www.authorhouse.com
Phone: 833-262-8899

Because of the dynamic nature of the Internet, any web addresses or links contained in this book may have changed since publication and may no longer be valid. The views expressed in this work are solely those of the author and do not necessarily reflect the views of the publisher, and the publisher hereby disclaims any responsibility for them.

This book is printed on acid-free paper.

ISBN: 978-1-4259-8315-4 (sc)
ISBN: 978-1-4817-2394-7 (e)

Print information available on the last page.

Published by AuthorHouse 07/30/2024

authorHOUSE®

Dedicated to

**My sons, Stephen Jr., Darryl, and Eric Fletcher
and
my grandchildren**

In Appreciation

I am deeply grateful to five people, without whom this book would not have been written.

**Mildred Parker – Provided me hope and encouragement to write this book
Ernie Simms – Good listener to read to, day or night
Gloria Bulluck – Gave me words of wisdom and was my first typist
Michelle Windsor – Special thanks for her expertise in the computer setup
Sondra Windsor – Made valuable suggestions for the book and typed the final copy**

Praise Him

**Giving thanks always for all things unto GOD and the Father
in the name of our Lord Jesus Christ**

Ephesians 5:20

I Thank God

I thank God for being the head of my life. Without you, I wouldn't be able to stand. You've brought me from a mighty long way. I can remember the times when I only had two pairs of shoes. One for church and another for work.

But down through the years, God still kept me in his care. And today I can stand and say where would I be if it hadn't been for God on my side. I thank God.

Now, I know more about God's word and how it has kept me. So I asked God to help me learn the Bible, and to understand what the verses are saying to me.

I started fasting, and things began to happen. With prayer in my life, I could remember the books of the Bible and verses.

Now I have learned the books of the Bible and have memorized twelve verses or more.

I thank God for who He is in my life, for when one door closes, thousands more open.

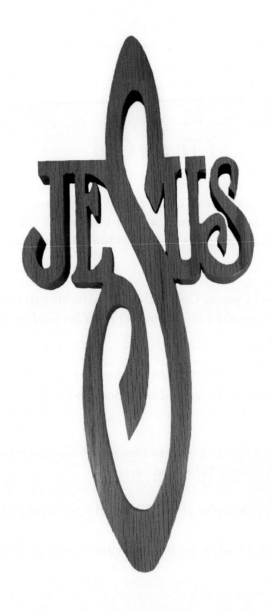

A friend loveth at all times, and a brother is born
for adversity.

Proverbs 17:17

He's My Friend

A Friend is someone who sticks close to you,
Helps you out with what you're going through
    He's my Friend.

So why sit feeling sad and blue?
Talk to Jesus, He will comfort you.
He'll be your Friend when no one's around,
So sing Him praises and rejoice now.

Trials won't last very long
When Jesus is by your side,
For His beauty is rare; you feel His presence everywhere.
    He's my Friend.

So don't just sit with nothing to do
Spread God's word, and make a friend or two.
Someone is waiting to hear your voice
So pick up the phone; or give them a call,
And be a friend.

So let's clap our hands and lift our voice in praise.

For Jesus is the sweetest name I know.

    He's my Friend.

The wilderness and the solitary place shall be glad for them; and the desert shall rejoice and blossom as the rose.

Isaiah 35:1

The Rose

She's the most beautiful flower of all;
I call her the rose.
The mother of all flowers.
Her colors: ruby red, pink, yellow, and white
Mix them all together; what a beautiful sight.

She opens with beauty so rare;
As her fragrance fills the air;
She's a mother, the rose, my dear.

Just watching her, holding herself so high,
Her long thorny stems; reaching the sky.

Bursting in her beauty; as people pass by
She's a rose; my dear, that's why.

So quiet and still; she began to lose her petals,
As she bows her head to die. For there is none
Like the mother flower, she's a rose, that's why.

Purge me with hyssop, and I shall be clean;
wash me, and I shall be whiter than snow.

Psalm 51:7

And his raiment became shining, exceeding
white as snow; so as no fuller on earth
can white them.

Mark 9:3

The White Blanket

One cold and blustery winter day
I dressed myself heavy and went out to play
Oh, what to my surprise: cold, white flakes
Falling down from the sky.

"Oh, what is this?" I said to myself,
"I can't stay out here all by myself."

The snow came down beautifully
Without making a sound
Within a few hours, it had covered the ground.

That's a white blanket, can't you see?
God changes the weather as He wants it to be.

Pretty and white, snow covering the ground,
I felt good before falling down;
Now, all cold and wet from the winter snow,
I must go inside now, by the stove.

For the earth is now frozen,
Making not a sound
The winter, white blanket has covered the ground.

For thou shalt eat the labour of thine hands:
happy shalt thou be, and it shall be well with thee.

Psalms 128:2

Recipe For Mother's Love

4 cups of happiness - 2 eggs well-beaten
1½ cups of peace - sugar that sweetens

2 cups of love - butter that richens
4 cups of consideration - flour that thickens

2½ cups of grace - milk that thickens
1½ teaspoons of wisdom - vanilla for flavoring

Blend all ingredients together
Pour into baking pan
Cook until well done.

Serve with joy and patience.

As the Father knoweth me, even so know I the Father, and I lay down my life
for the sheep.

John 10:15

Whereas ye know not what shall on the morrow. For what is your life? It is even
a vapor, that appeareth for a little time, and then vanisheth away.

James 4:14

Life

Life is not measured in hours or time,
For what's done for Christ lasts a lifetime.
Let not your dreams die or be bottled up,
For God can't use you all folded up.

Stretch out on God's word
And soar like an eagle in the sky,
For life is but a moment;
You live, and then you die.

By having peace of mind and encouraging others to pray,
You can live life to the fullest, each moment of the day.

To shew forth thy loving kindness in the morning,
and thy faithfulness every night.

Psalm 92:2

A Loving Mother

For the greatest love of all is that of a mother.
She understands when things go wrong and holds the family together.
God's got everything, "Mother," to cure your ills.
He'll give you strength and courage when things are still.

Though your beauty may fade quickly, and our hearts forget to care,
Mother goes on, on the wings of prayer.
When her moments are the darkest, and shadows do fall,
God holds mother's hands through it all.

For a mother's love is something none can give or explain;
It's not made up of emotions, but sacrifice and pain.
Nothing can destroy it, for her love stays the same.

When mother's heart is breaking, you will never know.
She kneels to God in prayer and He comforts her weary soul.
That's a loving mother.

So, if you have a tender message and loving words to say,
Don't wait until you forget; tell her today.

But thanks be to God, for which giveth us
the victory through our Lord Jesus Christ.

I Corinthians 15:57

Lord, I Thank You

I thank you, Lord, for the sunshine
and for the rain.
Thanks for feeling your touch, Lord,
over and over again.

Thanks, Lord, for letting me know
Just who you are, and for
Keeping me from going astray;
Blessing my heart.

I thank you, Lord, for food, shelter
and clothing, and everything
concerning me, for you've put smiles of joy where
no one else could see.

Each day when I awake, I stretch
out my hands to thee, for your spirit
of joy and peace is handed down to me.
Lord, I thank you.

This world I live in; you keep me safe each day,
traveling to and fro,
Sometimes not knowing the way
Lord, I thank you
For the word of God I share with others each day.

It keeps me from doing wrong
and shows others the way.
Lord, I thank you for good health and strength,
and eyes to see.

I thank you, Lord, again and again
for everything concerning me.
Lord, I thank you.

Song: You ought to take the time out to praise the Lord.

The voice said, Cry. And he said, What shall I cry?
All flesh is grass, and all the goodliness thereof is as the flower of the field:

Isaiah 40:6

Autumn Scenes

Just look out from your window;
See the beauty that meets the eye.
It's designed by God above
And bright as the morning sky.

The treetops reach upward
With the beautiful colors of Fall.
Birds singing so sweetly:
It's Fall, it's Fall it's Fall.

There are many scenes to see
You'll love and cherish them all.
But the greatest scenes of beauty
Are the colors of Fall.

Provideth her meat in the summer, and gathereth her food in the harvest.

Proverbs 6:8

Then saith he unto his disciples, The harvest truly is plenteous, but the labourers are few.

Matthew 9:37

Foods Of Color

Just plant some little seeds and make several rows;
Water them frequently and watch them grow.

Our foods have wonderful colors and are good to eat,
So select some of these, and you'll see.

Orange - pumpkins and sweet potatoes
Yellow - corn and squash
Green - spinach and kale
Brown - beans and rice
Blueberries, black cherries, and red apples, too.

So taste these foods of color
They are healthy for you.

The Lord bless thee, and keep thee

Numbers 6:24

God Bless Our Fathers

God bless our fathers on this special day. For a father's love is
precious in every way. He never leaves us feeling lonely or sad.
So just think how great it is to have a good and loving dad.

Fathers don't sit around, wondering what they can do, they're
always finding ways to make things better for you.
So God bless our fathers.

Our fathers try hard to smile when the cupboards are bare;
very little food for the table; no money to spare.

A father's love has no shape, no size, no color; it takes all of him
to fill the cupboards. He keeps on working through the cold,
heat, and rain, and God blesses him, again and again.

God protects our fathers when danger is all around, taking him
through the strong currents; only he returns back, safe and sound.
So thank God for our fathers, treat them special everyday.
God gave them to us, so don't turn them away.
God bless our fathers.

**Giving thanks always for all things unto God and the Father
in the name of our Lord Jesus Christ**

Ephesians 5:20

Lord, I Just Want To
Say "Thank You"

Lord, I just want to say "Thank You" for just these
three: the air, the land, and the sea.

For without the land, there would be no trees, no plants, no forest,
and nothing to feed.

For without the water, I would die of thirst and have
nothing to help clean or water the earth.

For without the air, I would not be able to breathe.

So I'll just say, "Thank You, Lord" for these three: the air,
land, and sea.

Now, just see yourself as a little flower that wants to
grow, with no air, water, or soil. But God stepped in
and gave us these three: the air, land, and sea.

Now turn the soil over and watch yourself grow. Up from
the soil, you can grow, grow, and grow.

It is God that girdeth me with strength, and maketh my way perfect.

Psalm 18:32

Our Strength In God

The Lord is our Shepherd
and our strength is in him.

He's our redeemer;
On him we can depend.

Our life is in his hands;
He promised to guide us all the way.

For we must live and love the Lord
and praise him every day.
He's our refuge and keeps us from all harm.

He gives us the strength and courage
when we lean on his everlasting arms.

In the beginning God created the heaven and the earth.

Genesis 1:1

And God set them in the firmament of the heaven to give light upon the earth.

Genesis 1:17

**And the Lord God formed man of the dust of the ground,
and he breathed into his nostrils the breath of life;
and man became a living soul.**

Genesis 2:7

God's Creative Hands

In the beauty of a snowflake
That falls from above,
God's creative hands are working, too;
Showing his mysteries and miracles of love.

What a loving God He is, to show us the
Mysteries and miracles from his creative hands.

Just for man to live on earth was God's master plan.
"He formed man from the dust of the ground, breathed on him;
and he became a living soul." Genesis 2:7

Man has every right to praise God, for He's in control.
For if there was no God; there would be no man.
So – so,
Let's praise God, everybody, for his creative hands.

For, behold, I create new heavens and a new earth:
and the former shall not be remembered, nor come to mind.

Isaiah 65:17

For we know that if our earthly house of this tabernacle were dissolved,
we have a building of God, an house not made with hands, eternal in the heavens.

2 Corinthians 5:1

God's Evidence

God gently folds the night away and
Breaks forth with a brand-new day.
From the sky above to the earth below;
His evidence is seen.

From bodies of water, to the waves at sea,
From the dew on the grass, and the leaves on the trees,
In the wind that blows, to the air we breathe
These are God's evidences seen.

I do set my bow in the cloud, and it shall be for a token
of a covenant between me and the earth.

And the bow shall be in the cloud; and I will look upon it,
that I may remember the everlasting covenant between
God and every living creature of all flesh that is upon the earth.

Genesis 9: 13,16

A Rainbow In The Sky

A rainbow came from heaven, full of colors,
Surrounded by a blue sky that made me wonder.

Could this be for me? I asked myself inside,
Or is it just a dream, which will soon pass me by?

It had to be a message sent from God,
Still watching over me, using his shepherd's rod.

Isn't it nice to know that God is still around,
Watching as he promised, and never letting us down.

And they said, Go to, let us build us a city and a tower,
whose top may reach unto heaven; and let us make us a name,
lest we be scattered abroad upon the face of the whole earth.

Genesis 11:4

Stair-Steps To Heaven

Prayers are the stair-steps to heaven,
Faith unlocks the doors.
Hope and courage, he will renew
Your strength when you trust God more.

Be still, and know that I am God: I will be exalted among the heathen,
I will be exalted in the earth.

Psalm 46:10

He Knows

No matter what your past has been,
you're not forgotten by God.

He knows your every care and need, and
he won't let you fall.

Trust God to work it out; just give
him the problem now.

He's loved you since the world began, so that
will not be a problem for him.

But if we walk in the light, as he is in the light, we have fellowship one with another, and the blood of Jesus Christ his Son cleanseth us from all sin.

1 John 1:7

Walk Right And Hold On

Winning Christ is the greatest victory
       that we can achieve.

To save a soul in times like these. Hold on.
       Opportunities to reach out to souls that are lost
       and tell them about a true and living God.

Help them to walk in the newness of life
       and warm their hearts on thoughts about Christ.

Man can't live by bread alone
       neither can he serve two masters and hold on.

For there are three anchors that hold fast
       one of faith, hope, and prayer.

Encourage yourself and others to hold on, for
       Christ is coming back, and it won't be long.

Now is the needed time to draw closer to God,
       for broad is the way, that leads you wrong.

For narrow is the way you must find that leads
       to eternal life with God. So…
       "Walk right and hold on."

Search me, O God, and know my heart: try me, and know my thoughts.

Psalm 139:23

Thought Of Thanks

There's a brand-new day before us and a chance to start; a new
And shining hour waiting to feed both you and me.

First
We'll gather around God's table and feast on the word, for no
One will be left out, all will be fed.
Thank God for the prayers that have been answered, throughout all the years.
We've shared with friends and relatives that needed to be fed.

For Thanksgiving is a time to celebrate, to bring togetherness and love,
Not to bicker and fuss, or to hold a grudge.

"So let's thank God!"

Thank God for health and strength, good eyes to see, for ears
To hear, and a mouth to speak.

Thank God for shelter over our heads, to rest at night in comfortable beds.
Thank God for fresh air, so we can breathe
Thank God for a sound mind in times like these
Thank God for the harvest time now that the crops are in
We'll have plenty to eat and feast on again.

"Now let's eat!"

The turkey has been sliced
The corn still in the pot
The peas in large bowls
Juicy and hot.
We've got mashed potatoes and gravy,
Ham and turnips, too,
Sweet potatoes and cornbread
And cranberries, too.

So gather around your table on this Thanksgiving Day and count
Your many blessings and give God the praise.

Yet if any man suffer as a Christian, let him not be ashamed; but let him glorify God on this behalf.

1 Peter 4:16

What Kind Of Christian Are You?

Some Christians are like wheelbarrows – they're just too good to be pushed.

Some Christians are like balloons; just filled with hot air, not caring about anyone but themselves.

Some Christians are like footballs, just bouncing around; they take no time out before lying down.

Some Christians are like kites, flying high in the air; they need their strings pulled when it's time for prayer.

Some Christians are like jumping water frogs; they need to stay cool, staying wet by the side of the pool.

Some Christians are like mocking birds, singing and keeping the beat; but when it's time for the word, they doze off to sleep.

Then there are those Christians that God has called to get the job done whatever the cost.

What kind of Christian are you?

Finally, my brethren, be strong in the Lord, and in the power
of his might. Put on the whole armour of God, that ye may be able to
stand against the wiles of the devil. For we wrestle not against flesh and blood,
but against principalities, against powers, against the rulers of the darkness
of this world, against spiritual wickedness in high places.
Wherefore take unto you the whole armour of God, that ye may be able to
withstand in the evil day and having done all, to stand.
Stand therefore, having your loins girt about with truth, and having
on the breastplate of righteousness; and your feet shod with the
preparation of the gospel of peace; above all taking the shield of faith, wherewith
ye shall be able to quench all the fiery darts of the wicked.
And take the helmet of salvation, and the sword of the Spirit which is the Word of God.

Ephesians 6: 10-17

Cry If You Want To

Many times in life, we make the wrong decisions, when
we should trust God and wait.

For trials will come on every hand, so don't give up or quit.
God will fight your battles, He will fix it for sure.

Now listen – Ephesians 6:10-17 tells us to put on the whole
armor of God. Fight with your helmet on -- that's salvation.

Cover your chest with the breastplate of righteousness and
shod your feet with the preparation of the gospel of peace.

Take the sword of the spirit, which is the word of God,

And above all ... shield of faith.

So, cry if you want to release some of that stress. God is still
working on your behalf.

He is not finished yet.

Behold, I stand at the door, and knock:
if any man hear my voice, and open the door,
I will come into him, and will sup with him,
and he with me.

Revelation 3:20

The Door

A shut door says "stay out,"
And an open door says "come in."
So don't keep the door shut;
Open it, so Jesus can come in.

But now they desire a better country, that is, an heavenly;
wherefore God is not ashamed to be called their God:
for he hath prepared for them a city.

Hebrews 11:16

Heavenly Place

There's a special place called heaven, that's far, far away, that we'll
reach someday; where many loved ones will be waiting and see us enter in;
A place where we'll rest forever, free from all worries and care.
All our troubles will be over, and we'll meet Jesus there.

For Jesus will light that city in the heavenly realm, and we'll be waiting
to see this heavenly place when we make it in.

**Because thy loving
kindness is better than life, my lips shall praise thee.**

Psalm 63:3

Mother's Love

M   Marvelous things that you have done, which made the race easier to run

O   Only one mother in the whole, wide world to give you her love when others fail

T   Tender love and care that you have shown throughout the years

H   Happiness that you have always shown, for if you're sad, no one will have known

E   Effort and good support, for you've shown up when no one else does

R   Remembering your mother brings lots of love, for God blesses mother each day from above

Two are better than one; because they have a good reward for their labour. For if they fall, the one will lift up his fellow: but woe to him that is alone when he falleth; for he hath not another to help him up.

Ecclesiastes 4: 9-10

My Friend Annie

How wonderful this world would be if more people were like you:
thoughtful, kind, considerate and understanding, too.

That's why it's always a pleasure just to say,
a person who's as nice as you deserves life's best each day.

A -   Accomplish the goals you set in life

N -   Nourish your mind with the word of God

N -   Never left alone when times get hard

I -   Increase our faith and depend on God

E -   Equipped and endure whatever comes your way

You're my Annie, no matter what's said

Basic Instructions Before Leaving Earth

And we beseech you, brethren, to know them which labour
among you, and are over you in the Lord, and admonish you;
And to esteem them very highly in love for their work's sake and be at
peace among yourselves.

I Thessalonians 5: 12-13

He's That Man
(A Tribute to Bishop Holmes)

He's a man who stands at the door,
With his head lifted up, saying "Yes" to the Lord.

He's not his own, he's been brought with a price;
He's a man that lives for Christ.

He's not ashamed of the gospel, and he preaches
loud and clear; says what he means, and means what
he says.

He encourages you to hold onto Christ; so anchor
Yourself; this man's right.

He has three anchors that hold him fast: one
of faith, one of hope, and one of daily prayer.

His love is like honey, sweet in the honeycomb;
His smile is like a flower in full bloom.

His footsteps are like a road map; going
from place to place. So, praise God for this man,
who we appreciate.

So now I am sure you know this man – none
other than Bishop Bobby Holmes.

All About Carolyn

Carolyn was born on December 10, 1945.

As a young girl growing up in the fifties, she had lots of things to do. She played with her doll, "Little Raggedy Ann," made mud cakes and dishes out of clay and other goods for her playhouse.

She loved going fishing and playing with tadpoles in the branch. Carolyn would swing on grapevines to get across the branch to bigger waterholes. She didn't mind getting muddy or wet; that was her way of getting out of work. Whatever the boys did for fun, Carolyn did also.

Carolyn enjoyed going to school and she had lots of friends. She had a special friend named Daniel Raggdall, but Stephen was her heart. She cherished everything he said and did.

Stephen and Carolyn saw eye-to-eye in togetherness, and things changed for them both, for the better, when they united as one and started a family. Carolyn has three sons: Stephen Jr., Darryl, and Eric.

Carolyn attended Douglass Elementary School and Frederick Douglass Senior High School in Croom, Maryland, where she graduated in 1965.

Carolyn started attending then joined the Deliverance Church of Christ in the 1980s. She received Christ as lord and savior in 1985 where she became a member under the leadership of Bishop Robert J. Patton. Carolyn also became a member of the adult choir.

Now, under the leadership of Bishop Bobby G. Holmes and First Lady Executive Pastor, Dorothy M. Holmes, Carolyn is presently a member of the welcoming committee at Deliverance Church of Christ.

Carolyn loves to write poetry and has a great love for children and senior citizens. Her hobbies are bowling, sewing, fishing, and writing poetry.

She has six grandchildren, seven brothers (four deceased), and four sisters.

Carolyn praises God for all he has done in her life daily and for giving her the opportunity to be a witness for him, because he deserves all the glory, all the honor, and all the praise.

Printed in the United States
by Baker & Taylor Publisher Services